Introduction

Welcome to **Famous People**, a unit of five programmes within the topic-focused series, **Stop, Look, Listen**, for 4–7 year olds. The series is sub-divided into two age groups, 4–6 and 5–7, offering teachers closely targeted support while exploring cross-curricular themes with their pupils.

Famous People is targeted at the 5–7 age group and focuses on history but also offers many opportunities for cross-curricular work. It will support the teaching of history at Key Stage 1 and also the Scottish National Guidelines 5–14 Social Subjects: Understanding People in the Past, stages P1–3.

In the unit, the lives of five people who have had a significant influence on modern-day living, are studied. Key events in their lives are depicted and questions about historical evidence of these events are posed. Teachers may wish to focus on the study of the particular person covered in a programme, or may wish to approach a programme with a view to covering the history component of a particular topic.

In addition to the teachers' guide, an activity book is available which offers many more opportunities for exploring the issues that surround each person's achievements. Also, five story books are available which offer additional support. See insert for details.

In addition to the focus on history and the exploration of a particular topic, the programmes offer a useful stimulus for a wide range of language opportunities.

Channel 4 Schools is keen to ensure that programmes transmitted are of a high quality and that support materials are well focused. We therefore welcome comments and suggestions about the programmes and the accompanying support materials. These can be sent to me at the address below.

Anne Fleck
Education Officer
Channel 4 Schools
PO Box 100
Warwick
CV34 6TZ

contents

About the series

The National Curriculum emphasises the importance of stories to provide narrative and accounts of what happened in the past. Stories can help develop children's awareness that the past is different from the present. Historical concepts such as cause and effect, and change and continuity can be introduced through stories.

Stories can provide a basis for work on other historical elements: chronology, interpretation of history, historical enquiry, and organisation and communication.

In **Famous People,** stories of the lives of five people are studied. Four are from the past, beyond living memory, and one is still living. They are **George Stephenson** (1781–1848), **Grace Darling** (1815–42), **Alexander Graham Bell** (1847–1922), **Mary Seacole** (1805–81) and **Neil Armstrong** (1930–). They have been chosen because their actions, experiences or inventions have had a direct influence on our lives today.

Each programme follows the life of the subject from childhood through to the main event for which they are remembered. As the storyteller/presenter relates the story, the key events are either dramatically reconstructed or, in the case of Neil Armstrong, shown through film. The presenter then visits an appropriate museum to try to find the answers to the questions: 'Is this story true?' and 'How do we know?'

Each programme offers:

- information about incidents in the lives of these famous people;
- historical clues and evidence;
- opportunities to see how life today has been changed by these people;
- opportunities to see why certain events happened;
- opportunities to ask and answer questions about the past.

The programmes

1. George Stephenson – Steaming Away

The railway engineer's story, culminating in the Rainhill Trials when Stephenson's *Rocket* won the day. The presenter visits the Railway Museum at York to see a replica of the *Rocket.*

2. Grace Darling – To the Rescue

The story of the lighthouse keeper's daughter whose dramatic rescue of survivors from the *Forfarshire,* wrecked on rocks off the Northumberland coast, is still remembered. The presenter visits the Grace Darling Museum at Bamburgh to see the boat used in the rescue and to examine newspaper reports of the event.

3. Alexander Graham Bell – Ringing the Changes

The story of the inventor of the telephone, leading up to his famous message: 'Mr Watson, come here. I want to see you.' The presenter visits Alexander Graham Bell's birthplace in Leith where she sees a replica of the original phone and also the patent issued to Bell.

4. Mary Seacole – Battling to Save Lives

The story of the Jamaican-Scots nurse, who financed her own mercy mission to the Crimea. The presenter visits the Imperial War Museum in London where many photos of the Crimean War are displayed.

5. Neil Armstrong – Man on the Moon

The story of how Neil Armstrong became the first man on the moon. The presenter visits the Science Museum in London, where she sees a replica of the moon landing craft, the Eagle, and the spacesuit used for the moon trip.

Teachers' guide

For ease of use, the notes for each programme have been arranged in the following sections:

Learning outcomes

This section states the aims of the programme in terms of the children's knowledge and understanding.

Programme outline

This gives information on the content of the programme – useful if you have not had time to preview it.

Key vocabulary

This section shows words that you may wish to introduce to the children before viewing.

Before viewing

These suggestions for preparatory activities and discussion are designed to help the children take a more informed view of the programmes.

After viewing

Activities are suggested to extend and develop the ideas introduced in each programme. These ideas are of varying degrees of difficulty and cover a range of curricular areas.

Background information

Further information is given on the subject of the programme, including a brief biography.

The guide also contains photocopiable worksheets for the children.

These notes are not exhaustive and offer only some of the ideas and activities which are possible. It is not intended for teachers to use all of them but rather for them to select those appropriate to their children's needs and compatible with their own interests, situation and teaching style.

In addition to the Teachers' Guide, an Activity Book, containing photocopiable activity sheets and accompanying teachers' notes, is available. This book gives children opportunities to consolidate and advance their understanding of human history.

Also available to support the series are five full-colour 24-page information books about the people featured in the programmes.

Recording and previewing the programmes is advisable. This allows you to use them creatively and integrate them into your work with the children. Viewing on video also offers greater flexibility for pausing at strategic moments. It is useful for repeat viewing, when pupils' attention can be drawn to particular events or decisive moments at key points in the drama.

Curricular links

The unit of five programmes has been designed so that it can be used as either a study of the lives of famous people, or the history component of a topic thus:

- **George Stephenson** – Transport
- **Grace Darling** – People Who Help Us – Lifeboatmen
- **Alexander Graham Bell** – Communication
- **Mary Seacole** – Health Education – Health and Hygiene
- **Neil Armstrong** – Space

Although the main emphasis is on history, there are many opportunities for cross-curricular work, for example, science, English, design and test, art, music, P.S.H.E., geography.

Famous People supports the study of history at Key Stage 1. It has close links with the Scottish National Guidelines 5–14 – Social Subjects: Understanding People in the Past, stages P1–3.

Relevant series from Channel 4 Schools

Stage One – Science for 5–7 year olds

Natural Inventions – Getting About – Jet Engines

Great Science Stories

I Want to Do That – I want to fly, I want to go fast

All About Us – P.S.H.E. for 5–11 year olds

Look After Yourself – Keep Clean

Stop, Look, Listen – Topic work for 4–7 year olds

Streetwise – Water For Life

PROGRAMME

1

George Stephenson – Steaming Away

Learning outcomes

The programme should enable children to understand:

- how steam locomotives were developed;
- how the first public railways were built and the problems involved;
- what life was like in the colliery homes of the North East of England in the early 19th century;
- why George Stephenson is known as the 'father of the railways'.

Programme outline

The programme opens at Rainhill, Liverpool, where the great train race of 1829 is about to start.

The storyteller asks the children to imagine what life would be like without railways. She then proceeds to tell the story of the 'father of the railways'.

She tells of George Stephenson's childhood in a mining village in the North East of England – how he can't read or write and how he has to go to work when he is only 10.

We meet George with his father as he sets out for his first day at work and find out how coal is all-important in people's lives at this time.

We follow George through to manhood by which time he is an engineer, very interested in steam power. He tries to interest a group of businessmen in his idea of a locomotive engine and passenger coaches running on rails. He develops this idea until finally he succeeds – the world's first passenger line opens between Stockton and Darlington with a passenger coach and 10 coal wagons pulled by George's *Locomotion.*

We next see George and his son Robert involved in a competition to provide the engine for the new Manchester/Liverpool railway. He is up against fierce competition but wins the day with his engine, the *Rocket.*

The programme concludes with the storyteller/presenter looking at a replica of the *Rocket* in the Railway Museum at York.

Key vocabulary

steam engine, coal mine, locomotive, passengers, rail tracks, competition.

Before viewing

▶ Talk about railways. Have any of the children been on a train? Where did they go? Ask for their comments on their journey. What did they like about it? What didn't they like about it?

▶ Talk through the process of rail travel – looking at a timetable, buying tickets, booking seats, waiting on the platform, choosing a seat, getting off the train.

▶ Explain to the children that there have not always been trains and that people used to have to rely on horse transport or boat.

▶ Make a collection of books and pictures about trains and railways, then and now, here and abroad.

After viewing

▶ Talk about safety on the railway. Remind them of the scene in the programme where the driver talks about kids trying to jump on the train. Design a safety poster.

▶ Revisit the story, reminding the children of the main events.

▶ Locate Stockton and Darlington on a map. Is there still a railway running there?

▶ Discuss and list the changes that the railway made to people's lives. Not all the changes were beneficial, for example to stage coach companies or workers.

▶ Begin a railway word bank. Draw an engine pulling wagons. Add the words as the train chugs round the classroom wall.

▶ Ask the children why coal was so important in the home. How was food cooked? How were homes heated? How did you get a hot bath? Make a 'then and now' chart showing heating, cooking, baking, and lighting past and present.

▶ Talk about George Stephenson. Remind the children of all the difficulties he faced. Why was he a very special person? What qualities and characteristics did he have which made him successful? What lessons can the children learn from his life?

▶ Have any of the children ever been on a steam train? Do they know what drives modern trains? Help them to complete Activity Sheet 1 by putting the trains in order of age. Give them a strip of paper so that they can stick the engines on and make their own time line.

▶ Help the children to complete Activity Sheet 2 by reminding them of what happened at the Rainhill Trials.

▶ If possible, visit a railway station with the children. Even better, go on a train journey with them. If this is not possible, then plan an imaginary journey.

▶ Set up a railway station corner in the classroom. The children can make up a timetable and fare sheet, set up a ticket office and print the tickets, lay out a railway coach and take turns at being the conductor. They could even set up a buffet, either on the platform or on the train.

▶ Start a book of railway/train poems.

▶ Ask the children to build a railway engine and track or bridge from reclaimed and recycled materials. They could paint a suitable backcloth to display their models.

▶ If you are fortunate enough to live near a preserved steam railway then this would be an ideal outing. If not, perhaps some train enthusiast would lend you a video of a steam engine at work.

▶ The children can make 'My Train Book' with engine shaped covers. In it they can write their favourite train poems, collect train and railway words, write a story about a train journey and illustrate them.

Background information

George Stephenson (1781–1848) was an English engineer and builder of the world's first public railway. He had never been to school but taught himself to read by attending night classes. He became a colliery engineer. In 1812 he was made engine builder at Killingworth Colliery near Newcastle. He spent the rest of his life designing and building railways and locomotives.

Between 1814 and 1826 he built a railway engine for pulling coal. In 1823 he was in charge of building a passenger railway between Stockton and Darlington. He himself drove the engine which pulled the first steam-hauled passenger train. He won the Rainhill Trials with the Rocket and went on to build railways throughout Britain, as well as locomotives for shipping all over the world.

He used the money from his inventions to set up schools for miners' children and night-schools for miners.

George Stephenson

A train time line

Cut out the pictures

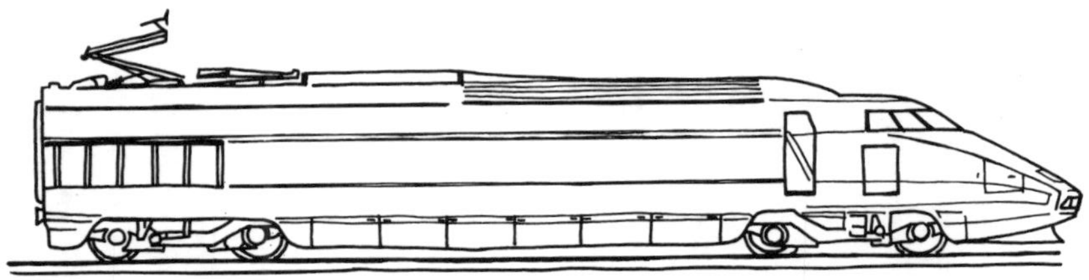

electric engine

the Rocket

diesel engine

steam engine

Put the pictures in order, beginning with the oldest railway engine.
Stick them on to a long strip of paper to make a train time line.

George Stephenson

The Rocket

Colour the boiler, water barrel, coal tender and wheels *yellow*. Colour all the rest *black*.

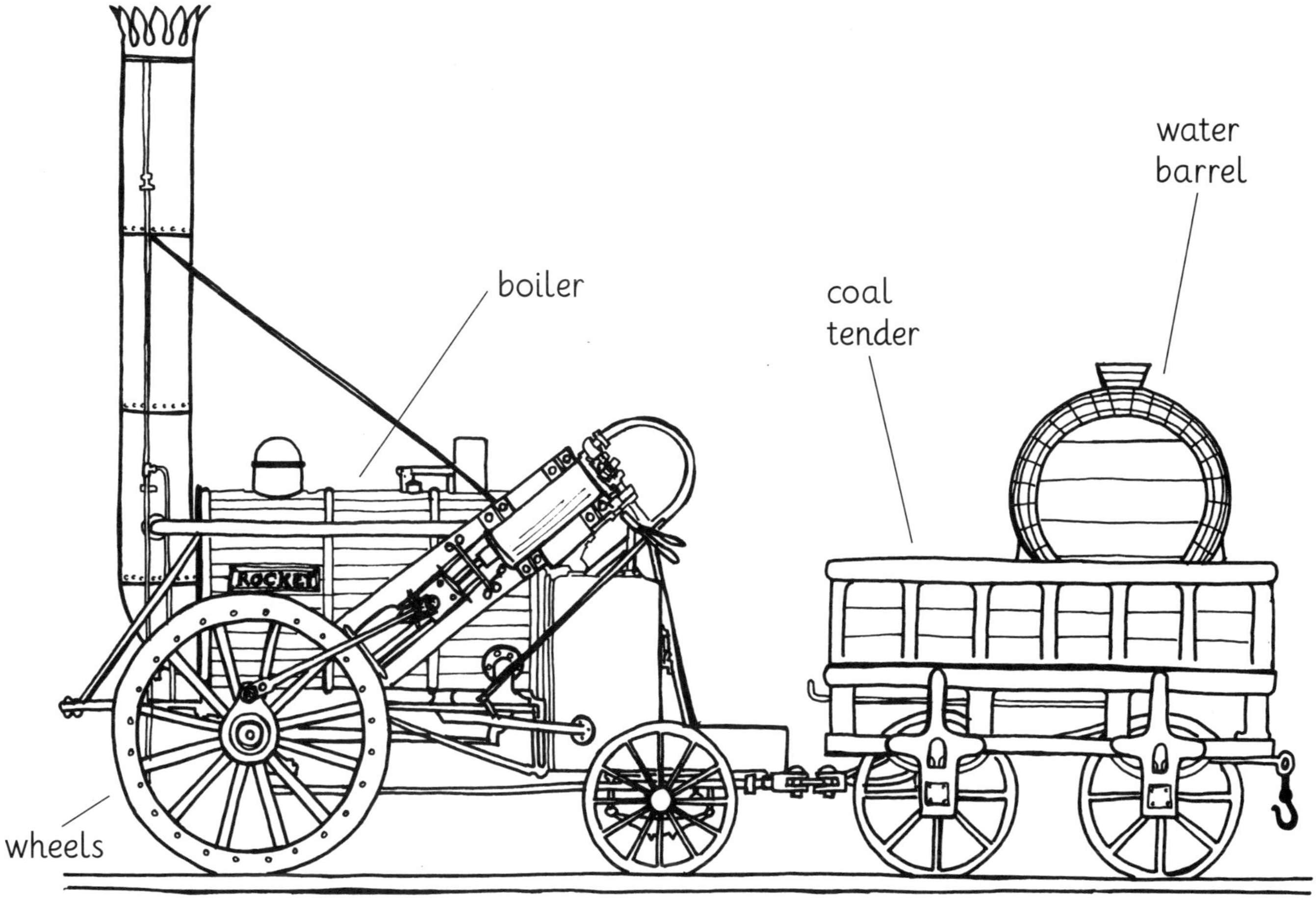

Join the words to make sentences.

This is	George Stephenson.
It was built by	the Rainhill Trials.
It travelled at	the Rocket.
It won	31 mph.

PROGRAMME

2 Grace Darling – To the Rescue

Learning outcomes

The programme should enable children to understand:

- the meaning of the words hero and heroine;
- how Grace Darling helped rescue nine people who had been shipwrecked;
- how we know about Grace Darling's daring rescue;
- how rescue at sea is organised, and the work of the R.N.L.I.;
- why we need lighthouses.

Programme outline

The programme opens dramatically with two survivors from a shipwreck seen clinging to a rock.

The storyteller describes the scene and then we see Grace begging her father to let her go to the rescue.

The storyteller then takes up the story of Grace's childhood as the daughter of a lighthouse keeper on Longshore, one of the Farne Islands. She enjoys helping her father with his work and by the time she is 22 she has become her father's assistant.

The scene changes to the sea where a steamship, the *Forfarshire,* is having trouble with the boiler. The situation becomes more serious as the weather worsens. The ship is thrown on to the rocks near Longshore. Most passengers are swept out to sea but nine manage to cling to the rocks.

Grace does persuade her father to let her help and they set out to the rescue in a fishing boat. Grace has the difficult task of keeping the boat alongside the rocks until some of the survivors are taken off. The story ends in the lighthouse kitchen with the survivors thanking Grace.

The storyteller/presenter visits the Grace Darling Museum in Bamburgh where she shows various 'Grace' artefacts.

Key vocabulary

heroine, bravery, rescue, lighthouse, lifeboat, storm, danger.

Before viewing

▶ Make a collection of books about lighthouses, lifeboats and 19th-century ships.

▶ Talk about dangers at sea and what happens when a ship is in trouble. Who rescues them? Discuss the work of the lifeboat service and the rescue work they undertake. Talk about the sort of boats used.

▶ Explain the purpose of lighthouses to warn ships of approaching dangers.

After viewing

▶ Ask the children if they think Grace Darling was brave. Why? Explain the word heroine. Do they think Grace was a heroine? Why? Grace's father had rescued many people in the past. Why do the children think that no fuss was made of him but only of Grace?

▶ Have the children ever been brave? Ask them to write about it and/or draw a picture.

▶ Discuss Activity Sheet 3 with the children and remind them of the events of that night.

▶ Act out the story of the rescue. Ask the children to imagine how the people involved felt. Help them to complete Activity Sheet 4.

▶ Make a storyboard of the events and caption it.

▶ Investigate lighthouses and their function. If possible, show children a sea chart.

▶ Locate the Farne Islands on a map.

▶ Grace was given a medal by the Shipwreck Institute, the forerunner of the R.N.L.I. Ask the children to design a medal to be presented to her.

▶ To help the children imagine the rescue night, discuss severe weather and storms with them. Have children experienced travel difficulties because of severe weather, for instance, not being able to get to school because of flooded roads or fallen trees? Have they experienced stormy ferry crossings? Talk about the wind. Have they ever been out in a really strong wind? What did it feel like? What were the difficulties? Nobody knows how strong the wind was on the night of the rescue. Discuss the Beaufort scale which ranges from 1–10. Children can invent their own wind scale or find a way of measuring the wind. A simple bunch of tissue streamers on a stick will do it.

▶ Help the children find out about the work of the R.N.L.I. Originally the Shipwreck Institution, it was founded in 1824 with the aim of providing a national rescue service for saving lives at sea. On the night of the rescue, a lifeboat had been launched from Sunderland but arrived after the Darlings' boat. Today there are lifeboat stations around the coast. Discuss how the lifeboat service has changed since the time of Grace Darling. Remind them that bravery and heroism haven't changed. Lifeboatmen are rewarded with medals for their bravery. Make a chart of 'then and now', comparing boats, lifejackets, communication, number of stations.

▶ Arrange a visit to a lifeboat station if possible. Point out to the children that the R.N.L.I. is a voluntary organisation. Are they surprised?

Background information

Grace Darling (1815–42) was the daughter of William Darling, the keeper of Longstone Lighthouse, on the Farne Islands off the coast of Northumberland. On 7 September 1838, the steamship *Forfarshire* was wrecked on the Harcar rocks about 1.5 miles from the lighthouse. The weather was so rough that the Darlings decided no lifeboat would ever be able to put to sea. So Grace and William set off alone in a rowing boat which really needed three strong men to row it. After a terrible struggle through stormy seas they reached the wreck and found nine survivors. Grace looked after the tossing boat while her father lifted the injured on board. Back at the lighthouse, she cared for them while her father and two of the rescued men went back for the others.

"Attentions and rewards were showered upon her. The Duke of Northumberland gave her a gold watch, the Shipwreck Institution voted her its silver medal, the Humane Society sent her a vote of thanks and its president a silver teapot. Seven hundred pounds were subscribed for her and boatloads of curious sightseers crowded the lighthouse tower. She was carried off by consumption in her twenty-sixth year. She was buried in Bamburgh Churchyard and so was laid to rest one of the greatest heroines the world has ever known. A memorial shrine was erected there within sight of the lonely lighthouse where she lived and died."

From *The Lifeboat* magazine of 1893, an article entitled 'A Noteworthy Jubilee'.

Grace Darling
A brave deed

Choose the correct word and complete Grace Darling's story.

1. Grace Darling lived in a ______________________________.
2. One night it was very ______________________________.
3. She saw a ship on the ______________________________.
4. She and her father rowed to the ______________________________.
5. They saved ____________________ people.
6. Grace was given a ______________________________.

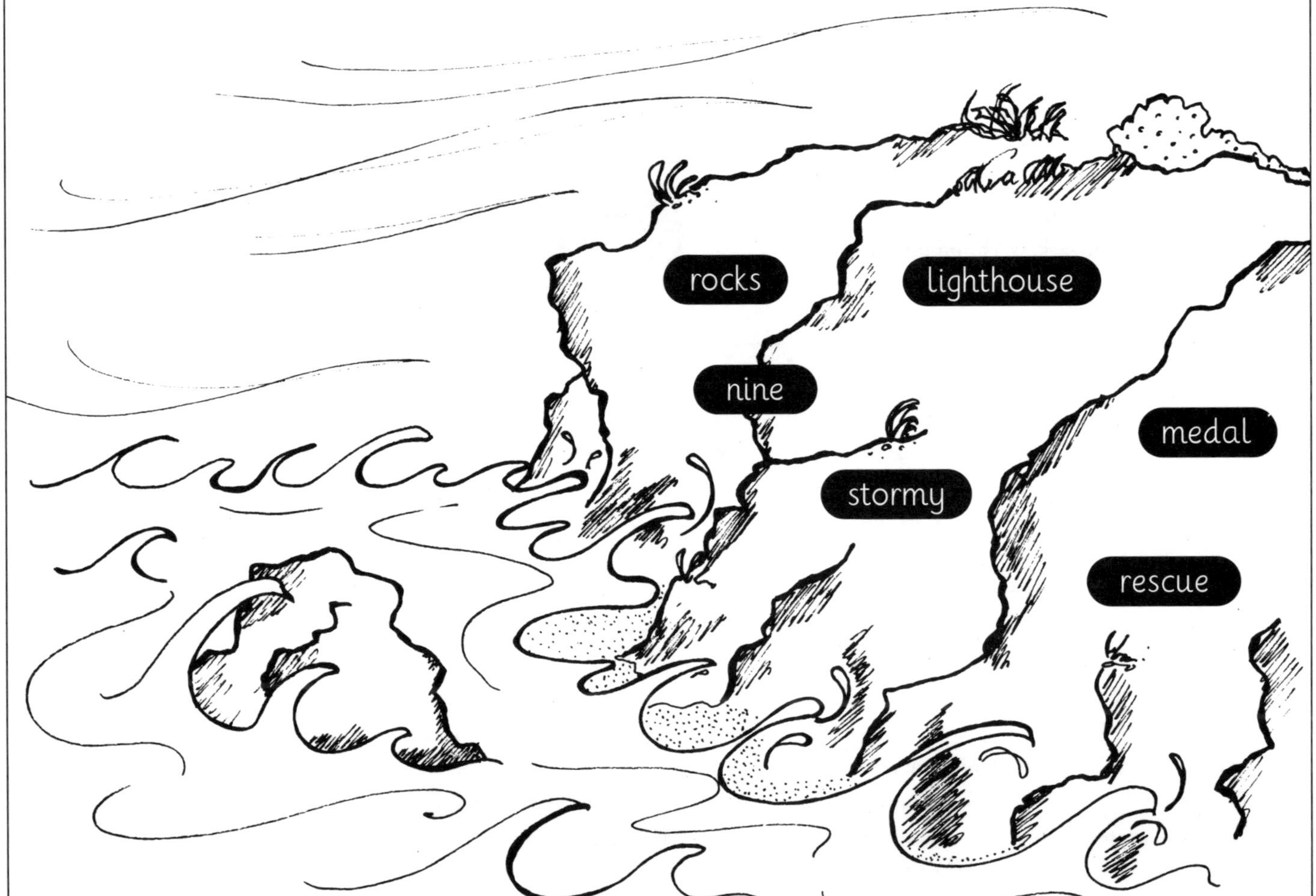

Grace Darling

After the rescue

What did they say?

Father

Grace

Sailor

Newspaper reporters

PROGRAMME

3 Alexander Graham Bell – Ringing the Changes

Learning outcomes

The programme should enable children to understand:

- who Alexander Graham Bell was and why his work was so important;
- the development of the telephone;
- the effect of the invention of the telephone on lifestyles over a period of time.

Programme outline

The programme opens very dramatically with Alexander Graham Bell consulting a medium.

The storyteller appears and introduces the story of Alex via a mobile phone. She recounts his early life and we see Alex with his family who all have an interest in the world of sound. Alex leaves Edinburgh for London to live with his grandfather, who introduces him to a speaking machine. This so enthuses Alex that he sets to work to develop his own.

After the premature death of his two brothers, Alex travels to Boston, USA, where he works as a teacher of the deaf. He still has a dream of inventing a machine that will allow people to talk to each other over a distance. He is encouraged by the invention of the telegraph but he wants to be able to *speak* into an electronic wire not just tap into it.

He sets up a workshop for his experiments and employs an assistant, Tom Watson. One evening as Tom is working on the machine, Alex hears what he calls a 'twang' from it. He sets up an experiment with a mouth-piece in one room and the receiver in the next room. Then comes the famous message: 'Mr Watson, come here. I want to see you.' – and Mr Watson does!

The presenter illustrates the development of the telephone from the Alexander Graham Bell Museum in Leith.

Key vocabulary

telephone, vibrations, telegraph, deafness, inventor.

Before viewing

▶ Talk with the children about telephones. Who has one? Do they know their home phone number? Why is it useful to have a phone? What would life be like without telephones? How would we communicate with people at a distance?

▶ Discuss the terms 'inventor' and 'invention'. Point out that inventions rarely come out of the blue, but are built on work done by others.

After viewing

▶ Ask the children why the invention of the telephone was so important. Make a list of the uses of the telephone. Which one do the children think is the most important?

▶ Although Alexander Graham Bell is remembered for inventing the telephone, he first made his name as a teacher of the deaf. He always thought of himself as a teacher of the deaf. Talk about deafness. Emphasise the loneliness and isolation of the deaf and the difficulty deaf or hearing-impaired children have in copying speech.

▶ Discuss communication over a distance in the pre-telephone age. Make a list of all the different ways it was used. These would include the pony express, mail coaches, runners, drum messages, flags, pigeons, ships etc. Talk about how communication over a distance has changed in the post-telephone age. Make a list of these changes. They would include faxes, e-mail, internet, voice mail, mobile phones etc. Compare the lists.

▶ Teach the children telephone etiquette: how to answer the telephone, how to take messages, and how to get someone to come to the phone. Talk about emergencies. What is an emergency? How do you dial 999? Rehearse this with a caller and an operator.

▶ Can the children think of times when a telephone has been a life-saver? Make a book or wall storyboard of such a time or event.

▶ Try this vibration experiment. Stretch cling film over a round tin. Sprinkle sugar on the top of it. Hold a metal baking tray above the tin and bang the tray. What happens to the sugar? Why?

▶ Work through Activity Sheet 5 with the children as they make their own telephone. Explain that this telephone works by sending sound waves or vibrations from the voice along the string. As the child talks into the cup or pot, the sound waves hit the bottom of the cup and make it vibrate. The vibrations pass along the string to the cup at the other end, shake the bottom of this cup and the sound waves reach the receiver's ear.

Remind the children that the string must be kept taut and that nothing must touch it. The cups should be held by their rims.

▶ Set up a telephone corner in the classroom, so that children can practise using the phone. Talk about dialing codes and numbers. Make an instruction card with them on how to make a call. Make cards with specific instructions such as: 'Phone a friend and ask her to tea' etc.

▶ Help the children to complete Activity Sheet 6.

▶ Collect pictures of old telephones.

Background information

Alexander Graham Bell (1847–1922), like other members of his family, trained to teach people to speak clearly. He went to America to continue his work and became convinced that he could teach deaf people to speak, even though they were unable to hear the sounds they were trying to imitate. He was also interested in other aspects of science and one of his experiments led to his invention of the telephone. He set up a company to develop and make telephones for sale.

After he retired from his telephone company in 1881, he continued inventing. One important invention was the 'vacuum jacket' – a device for administering artificial respiration. This was the precursor of the iron lung. Another interesting and life-saving invention was an X-ray device for locating bullets in bodies. This was used during the First World War and was instrumental in saving President Garfield's life after an assassination attempt. Another potentially useful invention was a device for lifeboats for condensing fresh water from fog or moist sea air.

Bell was fascinated by flight and experimented with kites and horizontally rotating propellers, thus anticipating the helicopter.

He also started the *National Geographic* magazine.

He remained modest and, despite his achievements, maintained until he died that he was a 'teacher of the deaf'.

Alexander Graham Bell

A telephone kit

Make your own telephone.

You will need:

2 yoghurt pots

2 used matchsticks

1 metre thin string

a pencil

1. Make a small hole with a pencil in the bottom of each pot.
2. Look at the diagram to check which way the pots go.
3. Thread the string through the pots.
4. Tie a matchstick to each end of the string.
5. Make a 'key pad' on each pot with coloured dot stickers.
   Write numbers on the dots.

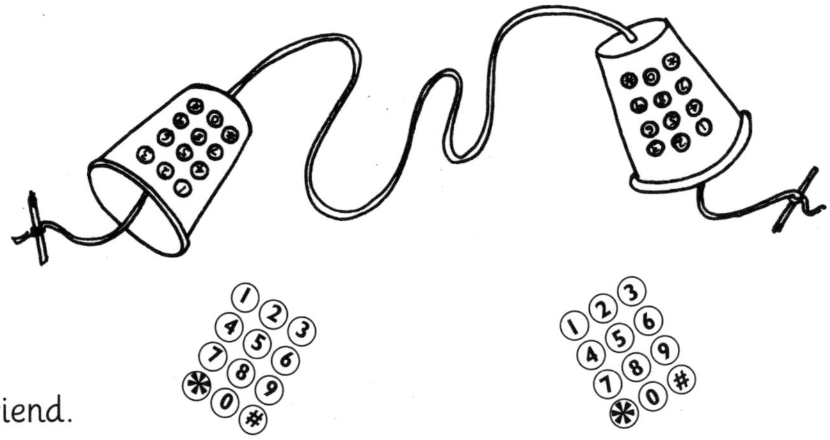

Now talk to a friend.

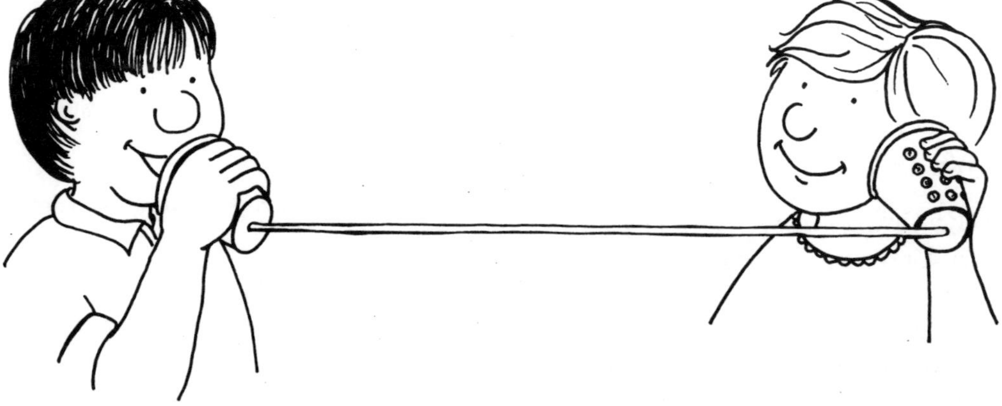

SCHOOLS

Alexander Graham Bell

A word puzzle

Find the telephone words.

z	r	c	a	l	l	s	f
n	k	i	d	i	a	l	g
n	u	m	b	e	r	p	t
o	j	h	e	l	l	o	y
v	r	i	n	g	u	c	a
j	m	e	p	h	o	n	e
x	h	a	n	d	s	e	t
c	w	m	o	b	i	l	e

PROGRAMME

4 Mary Seacole – Battling to Save Lives

Learning outcomes

The programme should enable children to understand:

- how Mary Seacole treated disease and wounds successfully;
- how good hygiene practices can make for better health;
- what hospital life was like in the 19th century;
- what conditions were like for British soldiers, who were wounded or ill during the Crimean War;
- how determination and commitment can succeed against the odds.

Programme outline

The programme opens with a wounded soldier on the battlefield, crying for help. The storyteller tells us that he is fighting in the Crimea and there are no ambulances or nurses, few doctors and none of the medicines of today. Who can help?

She opens the story book and begins the story of Mary Seacole, who was born in Jamaica.

Mary's father is Scots and her mother is a Jamaican who owns a small hotel where British soldiers and sailors stay when on leave. Her mother is interested in medicine and healing. Mary shares this interest and as she grows up she learns more and more about new medicines and treatments. She soon joins her mother in her medical work. She travels to Panama where she gains experience in nursing cholera victims. She is very aware of the need for cleanliness to stop the spread of the disease.

When Mary hears about conditions in the Crimea, she travels to London to offer her services. She is turned down – perhaps because of her colour. At her own expense she travels to the Crimea and sets up a 'hotel' (really just a collection of huts made from rubble) where she sells goods to the soldiers to make enough money to live on.

She nurses soldiers at the local field hospital. She realises the importance of good food and cleanliness in treating the sick and wounded. She works so hard that she makes herself ill.

The presenter then visits the Imperial War Museum and finds pictures of the Crimean War. She shows what happened to Mary on her return to England.

Key vocabulary

medicine, wound, bandage, disease, infection, nurse, doctor, cleanliness, hospital, germs.

Before viewing

▶ Talk about hospitals. Who works in a hospital? What do they do? What are hospitals for? Have any of the children been in hospital?

▶ Talk about the importance of keeping clean. Why do the children think it is important?

After viewing

▶ Ask the children why we remember Mary Seacole. Do they think she should be remembered? Why? Can they explain why Mary wanted to help the soldiers? What do they think we can learn from Mary Seacole?

▶ Invite a nurse in to talk to the children about their work.

▶ Now that the children have seen the programme ask them if the hospital they saw resembles one that they have been in. What were the differences? Make a comparison chart.

▶ Retell the story of Mary Seacole with the children. Then help them to complete Activity Sheet 7.

▶ Set up a Crimean hospital ward in the play corner. Beds and dressing-up clothes will all help to make the play more realistic and meaningful. Ask the children to suggest what else they will need.

▶ What happens when the children hurt themselves? What do we need to make cuts and grazes better? Talk about playground accidents. Then discuss the needs of the wounded soldiers in the Crimea. Help the children to complete Activity Sheet 8.

▶ Talk about the importance of washing hands. Ask the children to suggest when this is essential, for example after toilet visits, before eating, etc.

Make a wall chart with illustrations. The children could also make a notice for the cloakroom reminding pupils to wash their hands.

▶ The children could make a first aid box. They could decorate it appropriately. Discuss the contents. They can then collect empty packets of suitable items, such as plasters, gauze, etc.

▶ Find out about the life of Florence Nightingale – a contemporary of Mary Seacole's and also a pioneer of nursing care for soldiers in the Crimea. What was different about her experiences?

▶ Mary Seacole suspected that her black skin was the reason for being turned down by the War Office. This is touched on in the programme. You may want to pursue the issue of racism with your children. Ask them what they think of Mary being turned down because of the colour of her skin. Do they think this is a valid reason?

▶ Talk with the children about what happens when they are ill. Have they visited the doctor? Did they get medicine? Compare this with the treatment of the soldiers.

▶ Use a map or globe to locate Jamaica and Britain and the Crimea.

Background information

Mary Seacole (1805–81) was born in Jamaica. Her mother was black and her father was a Scottish officer with the British army in Jamaica. Her mother taught her African cures for tropical diseases and Mary became known as a 'doctress' in Jamaica.

In 1854 the British army was sent to fight Russia in the Crimean War. Mary went to England to join the nurses whom Florence Nightingale had taken to the Crimea. She was turned down, possibly because she was black, so she went out to the Crimea at her own expense and opened a store and eating place near the front lines. She showed great bravery, going among the men with medicines and supplies of food, bandaging the wounded and comforting the dying.

Both Mary Seacole and Florence Nightingale were greeted as heroines in Britain. Mary, lacking funds, wrote a book about her life called *The Wonderful Adventures of Mary Seacole in Many Lands* to raise some money. Soldiers collected money for a Seacole Fund which allowed Mary to return to Jamaica.

Unlike Florence, she was forgotten and died in relative obscurity in London. In 1973 a group of nurses erected a gravestone in St Mary's Catholic Cemetery, London, to commemorate her life.

Mary Seacole
Her life story

Tell the story.

Match the pictures and the sentences. Colour the pictures.

Mary sailed to England.

Mary was given a medal.

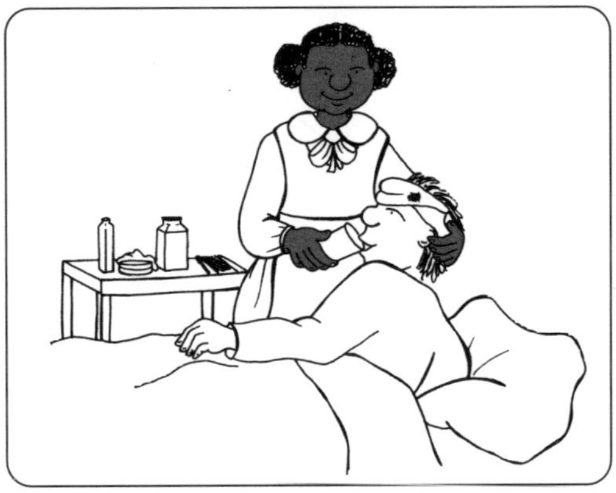

Mary helped her mother look after ill people.

Mary helped the sick and wounded soldiers.

Mary Seacole
Clean that wound

Cut out the sentences and glue them below the pictures. Colour the pictures.

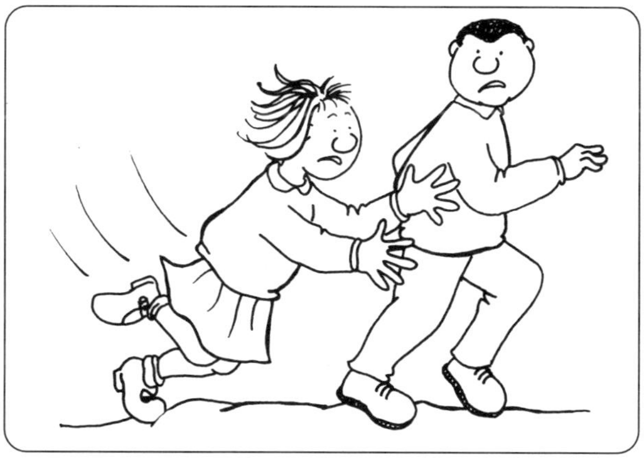

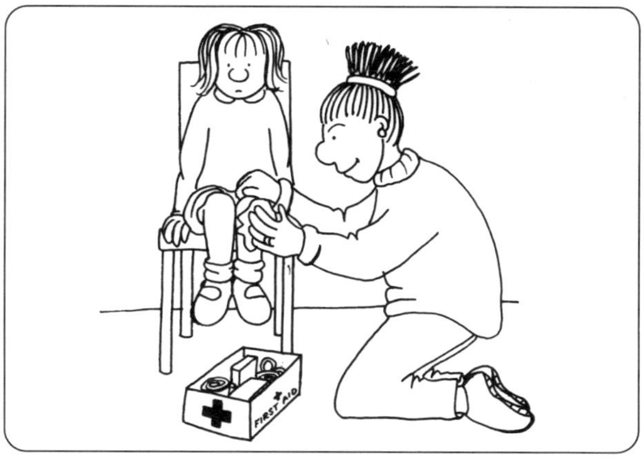

She has a plaster on to keep the dirt out.

She cut her knee.

Laura tripped and fell.

The teacher washed Laura's knee.

PROGRAMME

5 Neil Armstrong – Man on the Moon

Learning outcomes

The programme should enable children to understand:

- the preparation and training required by Neil Armstrong and other astronauts;
- what happened on the first moon landing;
- aspects of space travel.

Programme outline

The programme opens dramatically with the countdown to the Apollo 11 launch. The storyteller/presenter sets the scene for the story of the events leading up to Neil Armstrong being on the moonship.

We see Neil as a young boy having a recurrent floating dream. We see him being fascinated by aeroplanes and flying from an early age and later learning to fly before he can drive a car.

The moon race is on, President Kennedy wants an American to be the first man on the moon.

Neil joins the astronauts training with NASA. The training is long and hard. But finally the day arrives. Off to the moon. Neil finally lands in the lunar craft, the Eagle. He steps out of the craft. 'That's one small step for man, one giant leap for mankind.' He and a fellow-astronaut complete their experiments and then rejoin Apollo 11 and the third astronaut.

They arrive home to a hero's welcome.

The presenter visits the Science Museum, London, to see Neil's spacesuit and a replica of the Eagle. She meets Helen Sharman, the British woman astronaut, who talks about her eight days on Mir.

Key vocabulary

space, spacesuit, rocket, lunar, oxygen, gravity, spaceship, jet, astronaut, pilot.

Before viewing

▶ Show the children pictures of spaceships and space travel and discuss.

▶ Find out what they know about the moon.

After viewing

▶ Revisit the programme. Ask the children which part they found most interesting. Did they understand how the spacecraft had three parts to it and why this was: the lunar module for the moon landing, the service module to provide oxygen, water and power for the crew and, right on top, the command module, all of this mounted on to a Saturn rocket, the most powerful rocket ever built.

▶ The moon landing happened within living memory. The children can ask members of their families what they remember about the first moon landing. Have they any mementoes or souvenirs of the event?

▶ Talk about Neil Armstrong. Can the children explain how he became the first man on the moon? Do they think he was brave? Why? How would they feel being the first person to step out on to the moon? What sort of fears and worries might they have?

▶ Show pictures of the moon's surface. Make a model of the first moon landing. Talk about what they will need to include.

Help the children to identify the different tasks and list the materials required. Look at the spacesuit on Activity Sheet 9 for details of the astronauts' clothing. Copy the lunar module from pictures. The flag needs a stiffener as there is no wind on the moon. The surface of the moon with its rocks and craters can be made using either sand or papier mâché.

▶ Ask the children if they have visited Florida, where the launch took place. Locate it on a map or globe.

▶ Make a word bank of lunar words listed on a moon-shaped card.

▶ Make a book of moon poems. Some popular ones include 'Aiken Drum', 'The Man in the Moon', 'Hey Diddle, Diddle' and 'The Owl and the Pussycat'.

▶ Gravity is a very difficult concept for young children. Ask them what happens when they jump up. The reason that they always come back to earth is because of the Earth's pull or gravity. What happens to their tummy if they are in a car that goes over a bump or on a swing when it reaches its highest point? At these times they are momentarily weightless – just like the astronauts! Explain to the children how zero gravity in a spacecraft gives problems. It would be very dangerous to have things floating around inside. Can they suggest ways of overcoming this? What about food and drink? (Food comes in packages, held on a tray, fastened to the astronaut's leg, and drinks come in special containers which can be sealed after each sip.) Can the children suggest other problem areas and solutions?

▶ Ask the children why rockets are used for space travel and not planes. Space has no air. As you go higher above the Earth's surface, the air gets thinner and thinner until there is no air at all. You are in outer space. No air means that planes are no use, rockets have to be used.

▶ Look at Activity Sheet 9. Ask the children why breathing apparatus is needed. Where else is there no air to breathe? How do divers get air?

▶ Each astronaut is allowed to take his Personal Preference Bag or Diddy Bag as it is known. It measures 14cm by 12cm and has a string at its neck to pull it shut. Discuss with the children the things they would choose to take with them. Complete Activity Sheet 10.

▶ Act out the moon walkabout and all the tasks performed by Neil Armstrong: taking pictures, planting the flag, collecting rock and dust samples. They can make the equipment needed: flag, tongs, scoops and sample containers.

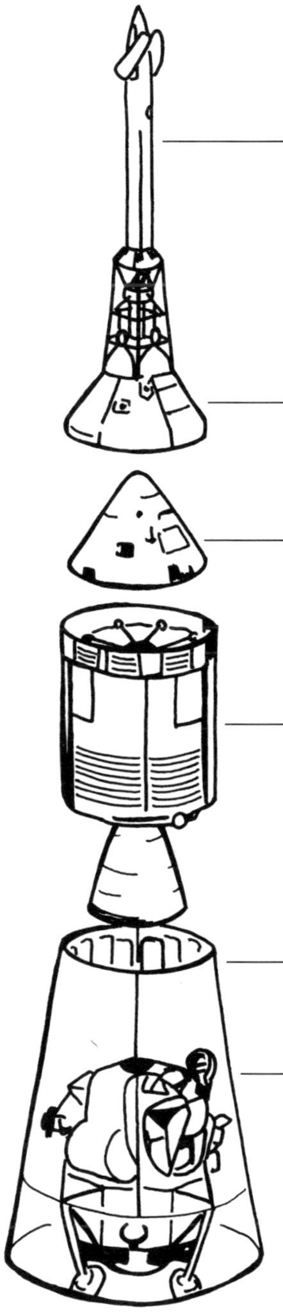

Cutaway drawing showing the parts of the Apollo Moonship and where it is mounted on top of Saturn V.

Background information

Neil Armstrong (1930–), as a young man, was always interested in flying. He earned his pilot's licence at the age of 16, before he had learned to drive a car. The following year he became a naval air cadet and went on to fly in the Korean War.

In the 1950s Neil became a test pilot for NASA (National Aeronautics and Space Administration) before joining the US space programme in 1962. In 1969 he joined astronauts Aldrin and Collins on the Apollo 11 mission, and on 20 July he became the first person to walk on the moon. As he stepped off the lunar landing module, he said: 'That's one small step for a man, one giant leap for mankind.'

Neil Armstrong
A space suit

Match the labels to the spacesuit.

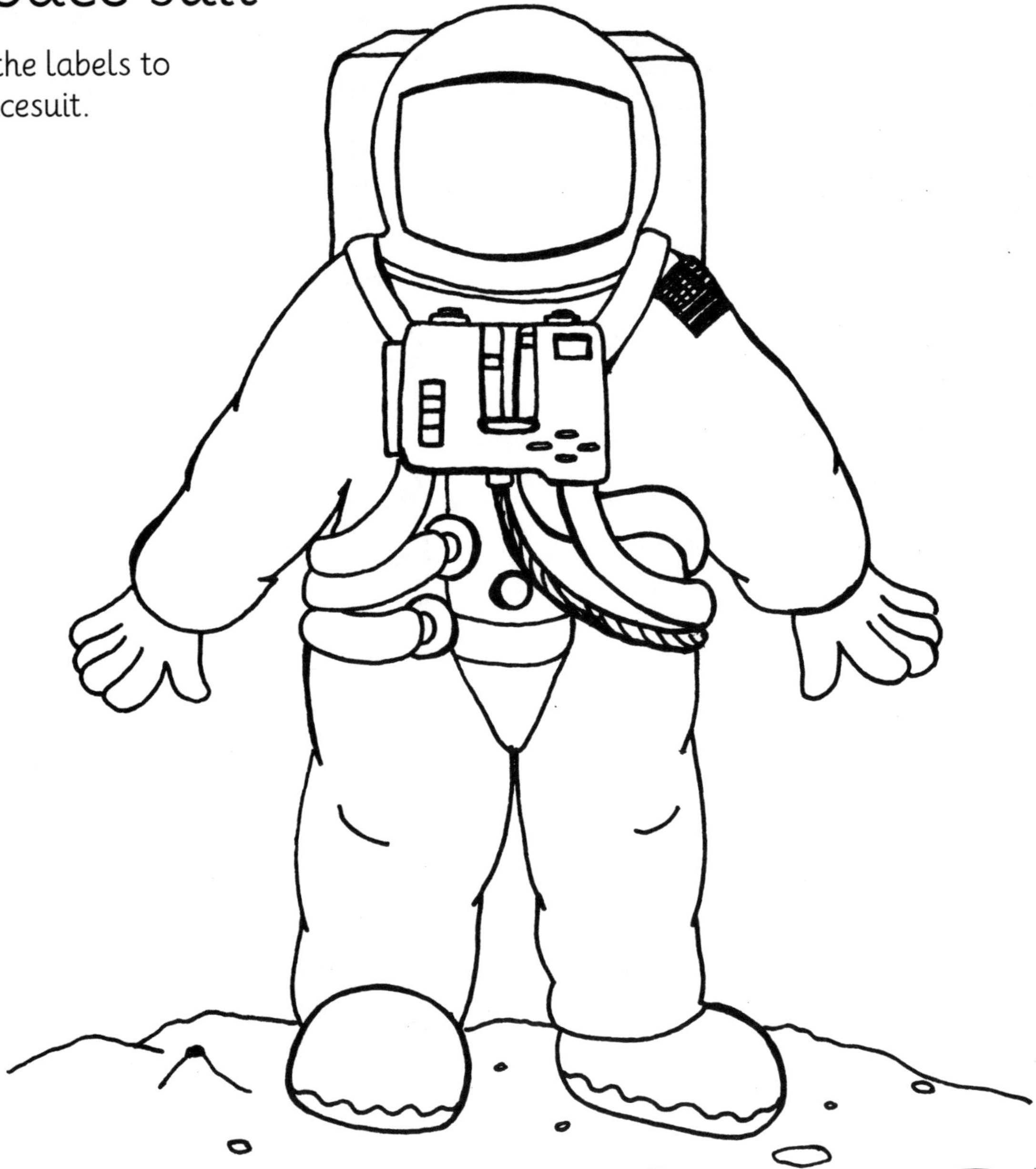

boots

gloves

jacket

trousers

life-support pack

helmet

visor

Draw your face inside the helmet.

Neil Armstrong
Your diddy bag

Decorate it. Draw what you will put in it to take to the moon. Remember the bag is small.

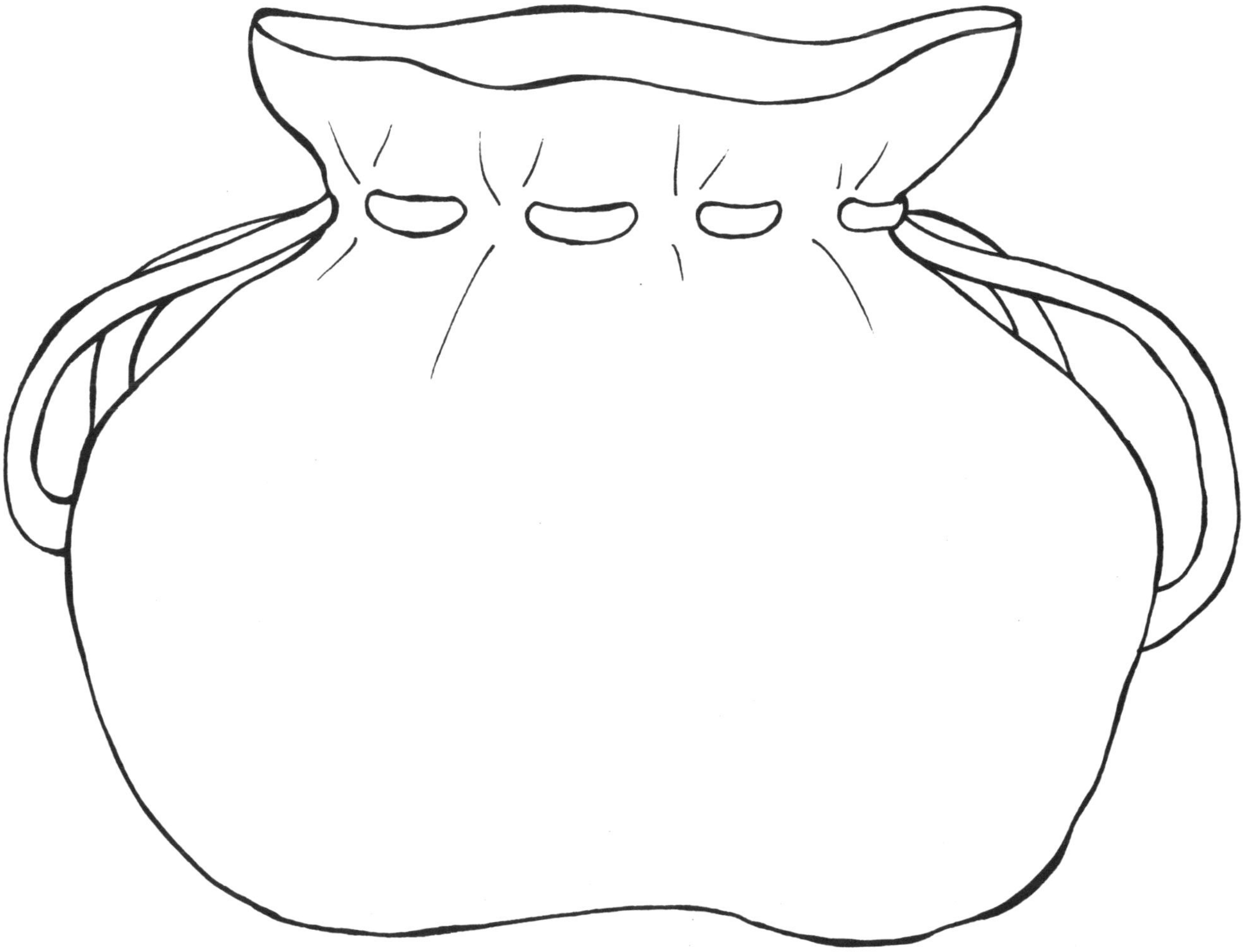

What I will take to the moon.

4 SCHOOLS

Additional resources

Famous People

George Stephenson

Young C. & King, C., *Railways and Trains,* Usborne, ISBN 0 7460 04672

Build Your Own, *Stephenson's Rocket,* Siena, ISBN 1 85813 4587

Story Book, *George Stephenson,* Channel Four Learning, ISBN 1 86215 346 9

Audry, W., *Trust Thomas,* Buzz Books/Heinemann, ISBN 1 8559 12902

Ahlberg. A. & Amstulz, A., *Funnybones & The Ghost Train,* Heinemann, ISBN 0 4349 60845

Grace Darling

*Cresswell, H., *The Story of Grace Darling,* Viking Kestrel, ISBN 014 054 1853

Armitage, R. & D., *The Lighthouse Keeper's Rescue,* Picture Puffins, ISBN 014 054 1853

*Ardizzone, E., *Tim to the Rescue,* Picture Puffins, ISBN 014 050 338 2

*Ardizzone, E., *Little Tim and the Brave Sea Captain,* Picture Puffins, ISBN 014 050 1754

Story Book, *Grace Darling,* Channel Four Learning, ISBN 1 86215 347 1

Technology Topics, *Ships and Shipwrecks,* Watts, ISBN 0 7496 1241 X

Alexander Graham Bell

Famous Lives, Usborne, ISBN 0 7460 30339

Stimpson, J., *Telephone Ted,* Ladybird, ISBN 0 7214 19186

Story Book, *Alexander Graham Bell,* Channel Four Learning, ISBN 1 86215 348 5

Mary Seacole

Seacole, Mary, *The Wonderful Adventures of Mrs Seacole in Many Lands,* OUP, ISBN 019 505 249 8

*Collicott, S., *Mary Seacole,* Ginn, ISBN 0602 247 829

Story Book, *Mary Seacole,* Channel Four Learning, ISBN 1 86215 349 3

Neil Armstrong

Technology Topics, *Space,* Watts, ISBN 0 7496 13270

Stott, C., *Space Exploration – Eyewitness Guides,* Dorling Kindersley, ISBN 0 7513 61089

Story Book, *Neil Armstrong,* Channel Four Learning, ISBN 1 86215 350 7

*Now out of print but still available at local libraries

Places to visit

The Florence Nightingale Museum, London, has information on Mary Seacole, tel: 0171 620 0374

National Museum of Science, London, tel: 0171 938 8000

The Grace Darling Museum, Bamburgh, tel: 01668 214465

Beamish Open Air Museum, Durham, tel: 01207 723 1811

National Railway Museum, York, tel: 01904 621 261

Stephenson Railway Museum, North Tyneside, tel: 0191 200 7145

Black Cultural Museum, Brixton, London, tel: 0171 7384591

Useful Internet Sites

http://nssdc.gsfc.nasa.gov/planetary/lunar/apollo11.html

25th anniversary of Apollo 11 - audio of rocket lift off, Armstrong's 'Eagle Has Landed...', 'One Small Step'

http://nssdc.gsfc.nasa.gov/planetary.lunar/lunartimelins.html

Lists all US and USSR successful lunar missions.

Lots to see on **http://nssde.gsfc.nasa.govsites**